'One In

C000245870

'A little book of the
abbreviations of the West Midlands

By

Michael Layton & Stephen Burrows

First published by Bostin Books in July 2018. This edition April
2020

(Find us on our Facebook page *'Bostin Books'* or website
www.bostinbooks.co.uk)

Dedication

This book is dedicated to all of our former police
colleagues, whose memories, wit and humour we
hope to have captured in this book.

Introduction

The nature of policing, with its adherence to rules and regulations, a strict discipline code, hierarchical rank structure, tried and tested procedures, and of course the rule of law, implies that formality must be the norm.

These principles can be evidenced no more clearly than by the four core pillars of policing, which are imprinted within the *'DNA'* of every police officer upon joining the service, and encapsulate the spirit of the role:

The definition of a Police Constable:

'A Constable is a citizen, locally appointed, but having authority under the Crown, for the protection of life and property, the maintenance of order, the prevention and detection of crime and the prosecution of offenders against the Peace.'

The Oath of Office of Constable in England and Wales, sworn by every police officer before a Magistrate:

'I do solemnly and sincerely declare and affirm that I will well and truly serve the Queen in the office of constable, with fairness, integrity, diligence and impartiality, upholding fundamental human rights and according equal respect to all people, and that I will, to the best of my power, cause the peace to

—

be kept and preserved and prevent all offences against people and property, and that while I continue to hold the said office I will to the best of my skill and knowledge discharge all the duties thereof faithfully according to law'

The formal caution - old and new:

'Do you wish to say anything? You are not obliged to say anything unless you wish to do so but whatever you say will be taken down in writing and may be given in evidence'

*

'You do not have to say anything. But, it may harm your defence if you do not mention when questioned something you later rely on in court. Anything you do say may be given in evidence'

The Oath taken at Court before giving evidence:

'I swear by Almighty God that the evidence I shall give will be the truth, the whole truth, and nothing but the truth'

***

Notwithstanding the formalities which have to be adhered to when working in an operational environment, the police service, in keeping with many other occupations, has developed its own sub-language and culture which has been transformed and added to over many decades.

The authors of this little book were born in Birmingham, and worked in the police in the City, and the wider West Midlands, during their extensive service, spanning more than seventy years. Having already explored the world of so-called *'Brummie'* slang words, in a previous book, they have now taken a light-hearted look at the slang, nicknames and abbreviations commonly in use in the police from the days before *'political correctness'* to the present day, assisted by the memories of more than fifty colleagues, both serving and retired. Some of these have been adopted from sayings from outside the 'Job', but the majority form a language of their own.

Viewed through the prism of today's society one might be forgiven for thinking that some of the material is rather devoid of the *'political correctness'* now seen in more modern times. The authors do not seek to defend its use but rather to present it *'warts and all'* as a piece of social history.

'Black Humour' is a facet of police culture and in truth it is probably one of the many 'coping mechanisms' which enable staff to function in a job which can be hugely stressful, often unpredictable and violent, as well as routinely challenging. Many police slang phrases embrace an element of *'darkness'* but rarely are, or were intended to be

—

4

malicious or negative. In an environment where most gave 'as good as they got' the word 'banter' was quite commonly heard.

Members of the public coming across snippets of this slang might be amused at its wit, or shocked at its sometime sharpness, bluntness or apparent lack of feeling, but it is an important part of police culture and history. Humour in the face of tragedy, death, violence, despair and degradation is, without a doubt, a normal human response, and until experienced, is not easily understood by the outsider.

So we ask the non-police reader to bear this in mind. You may be shocked by some of the older sayings, which we include for the sake of historical completeness, but which are now rightly consigned to history.

Above all enjoy the humour, and the window it provides into a secret world, because this book is also a historical document, preserving this language before it fades from memory.

***

For simplicity, this collection of over five hundred phrases, nicknames and abbreviations is presented in alphabetical order, using of course the phonetic alphabet still routinely employed by officers and police staff to this day.

—

A – Alpha

'A1 Intel' – very reliable information – this emanates from the police grading system for intelligence.

'A.C.C.' – Assistant Chief Constable – the first 'Chief Officer' rank.

'A.C.P.O.' – the Association of Chief Police Officers – the staff association for officers above Chief Superintendent rank.

'AES' – Accident Enquiry Squad.

'A.F.O.' – Authorised Firearms Officer – all volunteers, and extremely skilled. They are also drawn to wearing black jumpsuits, festooning themselves with equipment, and smashing doors into matchwood!

'A.N.P.R.' – Automatic Number Plate Recognition.

'A.R.D.' – Additional Rest Day – a product of the old *'earlies, lates and nights'* shift system, which had to have a floating rest day to work properly. Beloved of the station overtime champions because working one of these attracted double time in terms of payment and a day off in lieu if insufficient notice was given of a requirement to work it.

'ASB' – Anti Social Behaviour – thus, **'ASBO'** – Anti Social Behaviour Order.

'A.T.S.' – Anti Terrorist Squad.

'A.W.O.L.' – absent without official leave from the military.

'Across the pavement job' – an armed robbery on a stationary security vehicle delivering cash – a regular scenario in *'The Sweeney'* TV series.

'Acting' – temporarily promoted. A period of *'Acting'* is usually prefaced by some sort of statement about gaining 'useful experience' by the *'gaffer'*, but often actually means, *'we are so short of people and you are the closest to the real thing we've got'*. Still, you get extra pay!

'Afters' – drinking after permitted licensing hours.

'Aladdin's cave' – a criminal's house full of stolen property.

'All correct sir' – words of introduction by an officer upon meeting an Inspector or above.

'Ambo' – ambulance – the thing an officer wants to see most when someone is bleeding profusely in front of them and they are trying to remember their First Aid training!

'Anacapa' – the brand name of a method of criminal intelligence analysis – the original training required people to draw charts on rolls of wallpaper but now the process is computerised.

'Appointments' – a very traditional concept. In the *'good old days'*, when *'apple scrumpers'* were clipped around the ear, and the police were much more military in structure and style, the pre-shift *'parade'* was an actual parade and inspection. As part of this event officers were expected to produce, and hold up, their *'appointments'*, comprising of truncheon, handcuffs and pocketbook, for inspection prior to commencing duty. The name *'parade'* has stuck, although it is now more of a briefing, and the production of these items is no longer celebrated.

Figure 1: Appointments

'A pull' – to stop someone for questioning or search – also known as **'a tug'**. It applies to both vehicles and persons.

'Arly Barly' – it's for real and not a **'wind up'** –

otherwise known as *'no plonky plonky'*, *'official'*, or *'official no blag'*.

'A right stack up' – a big fight.

'Auntie' – the illicit local girlfriend of an officer–also known as *'a bit on the side'*.

***

B – Bravo

'B.D.H.' – burglary dwelling house.

'BINGO seat' – the seat furthest from the door in a police van – it stands for, *'Bollocks I'm Not Getting Out'*.

'B.O.N.G.O' – a nickname for any officer who avoided going out on patrol – it stands for *'Books On Never Goes Out'*

'B.O.P.' – Breach of the Peace.

'Bag someone' – to breathalyse someone.

'Bag of rats' – a messy situation. This is usually applied to an incident that isn't running smoothly, easily resolved or looks like it's going to involve lots of paperwork.

'Bagman' – acting as an assistant to a senior officer/investigating officer – although it carries with

it some responsibilities it can be the ticket to some interesting trips.

'Balls it up' – to make a mistake.

'Bandit country' – a West Midlands Police reference to the surrounding rural areas in particular, Warwickshire and Worcestershire.

'Bandit vehicle' – the offender's vehicle in a pursuit situation.

'Banged to Rights' – caught red-handed – unfortunately this situation often still results in a *'full and frank denial'*, resulting in time-consuming court proceedings, before a 'guilty' plea is proffered at the last minute.

'Banged up' – in a cell, or in prison – believed to derive from the noise made by the heavy cell door shutting, which is usually maximised by a robust pull of the door from an officer to make sure that it is loudly shut as the alleged miscreant enters for a period of contemplation of his or her wrongdoing.

'Banter' – a jokey and humorous interchange.

'Barking up the wrong tree' – looking for the truth in the wrong direction.

'Barny' – a row or argument.

'Batman' – an officer who habitually wore a police cape – the best thing about the much- beloved and still mourned cape was the fact that a bag of chips could be safely secreted from view beneath it and consumed whilst on *'stationary observations'* in an alleyway or doorway. A surprising number of criminals have been accidentally arrested by this method!

'Batting for England' - said of an *'expert'* who attended jobs but never did any paperwork as a result. These *'skilled operators'* were much in demand with harassed Controllers on the radio and would be given lots of trivial incidents to finalise. They were also favourites in the station front office as they were able to solve nearly all front-counter problems without picking up a pen, exercising any legal powers or causing inconvenience to colleagues and supervisors.

'Behind the door' – a prisoner in a cell.

'Bender' – a suspended prison sentence - always a delight for an officer to find that a difficult prisoner was the subject of one of these, as you knew they were going to prison as a result of being in breach of a previous court sentence.

'Bending someone's ear' – engaging them in animated conversation.

'Bent as a banana/as a nine bob note' – corrupt.

'Big Issue' – Force Standing Orders.

'Bilking' – making off without payment.

'Billy no mates' – someone who is not popular.

'Birmingham screwdriver' – a hammer.

'Bins' – spectacles.

'Black Dog' – the excuse often given for having an accident in a police vehicle, that a dog had run in front of the officer's vehicle and caused them to swerve. The mystery dog always ran off afterwards. Occasionally the dog was reported as being a fox!

'Black Half Crown' – using a police warrant card to get into nightclubs free of charge. A practice which has been much frowned upon in more recent years as being inappropriate.

'Blacksmiths boy' – a young male, tall and well-built.

'Black Rover' – the nickname for a Warrant Card, when used to obtain free entry or other goods and services in the old days.

'Blagging' – an armed robbery.

'Blagging' – playing the fool with police colleagues and trying to play tricks on them. The *'wee small hours'* in particular, when all was quiet, were favourite times for some quite elaborate tricks such as the *'cycling proficiency test'* for probationers in order that they could *'recover stolen bicycles'*. These would be held in the back yard of a police station over a course of traffic cones and officiated by a Sergeant with a blank clipboard. Another one entailed handing the youngest officer on the shift two table tennis bats and putting him on the Coventry Road to await an aircraft that was in distress and needed signalling to land safely. There were hundreds, thousands, of pranks played, enough for another book....

'Block' – the cell block

'Blister' – a traffic ticket.

'Blister' – an officer who turns up after all the hard work is done. (Often apportioned to the CID)

'Blower' – landline telephone.

'Blown it' – failed in an attempt to do something.

'Blues and twos' – a police vehicle with its blue lights on and siren sounding.

'Body' – a prisoner.

'BOHICA' – whenever yet another Force reorganisation was announced – *'Bend Over Here It Comes Again'*.

'Bollocking' – a telling off.

'Bonnet' – hair.

'Boss!' – what every prisoner shouts through the cell hatch to attract the Custody Officer's attention.

'Boy Racers' – drivers of *'souped up'* cars at urban unofficial racing events.

'Bracelets' – handcuffs.

'Bradawl' – an affectionate nickname for an uninteresting member of the shift i.e. *'boring tool'*.

'Brass' – a prostitute otherwise known as a *'lady of the night'*.

'Break' – a burglary.

'Brief' – a solicitor or barrister.

'Bronze' – codename for a tactical level police commander at in incident or event.

'Brown bread' – dead.

'Bullshit baffles brains' – talking rubbish to try and convince people that you know best.

'Bunch of knuckles' – a punch.

'Bungalow' – a person with 'nothing up top'.

'Bunny boiler' –a female who, once scorned after a brief liaison, seeks vicious revenge – taken from the film *'Fatal Attraction'*.

'Burgess check' – a check of the electoral register in the days before everyone happily put all of their details on the internet for Google to know!

'Bus Drivers trousers' – un-ironed uniform trousers – the absolute worst are generally dog- handler's trousers, which are rarely ironed, and usually sport copious amounts of dog hair.

***

C – Charlie

'C.I.' – a Chief Inspector.

'C.I.D.' – Criminal Investigation Department.

'C.M.P.G.' – Central Motorway Police Group.

'C.P.O.' – Crime Prevention Officer.

'CRO' – a person with a criminal record – it stands for Criminal Records Office. One of the most widely used terms in policing, as in, *'he's CRO'*.

'CRO74' – offender's descriptive form.

'Cacs/caks' – a derogatory term by Birmingham officers about fellow officers in Coventry, based on the car registration numbers of some of the police vehicles deployed there.

'Call it in' – call other officers in to make or assist in an arrest, or provide prisoner transport – remember that, *'Once Upon a Time, in a Galaxy Far, Far, Away'*, police officers actually walked around and needed a car or van to take prisoners to the *'nick'*.

'Can't lie straight in bed' – an habitual liar.

'Cardboard Cut-Outs' – officers at football matches who watch disorder from a distance, rather than getting *'stuck in'*.

'Carry on sir' – formal and old-fashioned words said to an Inspector or above by an officer upon leaving their company.

'Cat A' – high-risk prisoner.

'Check their happy sack' – to check someone's bag for stolen property if they were known burglars or shoplifters.

'Chicken' – a Punk Rocker wearing a resplendent hair display.

'Chief Supt.' – Chief Superintendent. Often called many other things!

'Ching' or *'Ker Ching'* – extra money earned as a result of working overtime – comes from the sound made by a cash register.

'Chokie' – the cells.

'Chop shop' – a criminal's site for dismantling and rebuilding stolen vehicles with new identities.

'Chummy' – a prisoner.

'Civil Matter' – something that doesn't require police action – often used to *'cuff'* a job to prevent further paperwork. The incident log was usually closed with the immortal words, *'civil matter, all parties advised'* and no further elucidation was ever required.

'Clink' – prison.

'Coffin' – an officer who is a dead weight and takes six others to carry them.

'Coffin Nail' – a cigarette.

'Coke' – cocaine.

'Collar' – to make an arrest.

'Collar Number' – individual police number worn on epaulettes.

'Community car' – an old vehicle without registered

owner or documents used by various local criminals and left parked for general use.

'Comp Grant' – the annual repayment of tax on rent allowance – dates well back into police history when large numbers of officers had accommodation provided. This meant that those officers who provided their own accommodation received a monthly 'rent allowance' in lieu of a 'free' house. This was a tax-free allowance, but taxed, monthly at source. *'Compensatory Grant'* was the annual repayment of this tax in April each year, and could amount to a significant lump sum. It was phased out many years ago after police pay was rationalised and lots of ancient allowances were absorbed into normal pay. Many an officer would try and hide this useful lump sum from their spouse and redirect it towards their own selfish pursuits. One wag used to tell his wife, every year, that he had, 'paid the compensatory grant and that she should not worry.'

'Coppers nark' – an informant.

'Cop a plea' – getting a *'guilty plea'* at court from a defendant. One officer recalls a case where a defence barrister made a plea to the Judge for his client to be given a sentence in months, rather than years, due to his guilty plea. The judge complied by sending the defendant to prison for thirty-six months.

'Cottaging' – importuning for an immoral purpose by homosexual men in public toilets or meeting place. Derives from Victorian times when many public toilets looked like little 'cottages'.

'Cough' – an admission of guilt, by a defendant, to an offence during a police interview.

'County Wankers' – a reference to police officers working in county areas.

'Creepy Insect Department' – CID.

'Crimsec Forms' – crime data forms.

'Cruel C's' – the 'C ' Division section of the Operational Support Unit.

'Cuff' – to handcuff someone.

'Cuff it' – to not deal with something properly.

'Cushy number' – a nice comfortable job that doesn't take too much effort.

***

D – Delta

'D & D' – drunk & disorderly.

'D & I' – drunk and incapable.

'DCI' – Detective Chief Inspector.

'D.K.F.' – door knocking feather – for when you didn't want the door answering.

'D.O.A.' – dead on arrival at hospital.

'D.P.' – detained property – an ever-increasing hoard of articles that often refuses to be got rid of, due to pending court cases, many months and even years old, and officers moving and forgetting, or failing, to return it after court. Detained property generally grows relentlessly filling rooms and basements and can sometimes lead to the downfall of officers for not following correct procedures.

'D.P.T.C.' – District Police Training Centre – for many years the centre at Ryton on Dunsmore near Coventry, provided initial recruit training for surrounding police forces.

'D.S.Bs' – Dirty Shitty Bikers / Hell's Angels.

'D.S.U' – Digbeth Special or Support Unit. The name slightly altered over the years. A very successful unit originally set up in 1979 to tackle street crime in Birmingham City Centre.

'Dabs' – fingerprints – derives from the *'dabs'* of ink used to take them.

'Dawn chorus' – the sound of *'farts, burps and*

groans' at 05.45 am briefing. They were especially tuneful after a couple of pints and a curry the night before.

'Dealer' – a person concerned in the supply of controlled drugs.

'Depth charge' – nickname for an officer with deep pockets who is always looking for a 'sub'.

'Dingly Dell' – cell.

'Dinosaur' – someone who is not receptive to change.

'Dipper' – a thief who *'picks pockets'*.

'Dipstick' – a fool.

'Dizzie driver' – disqualified driver.

'Do a Donald' – exit quickly – connected to the character *'Donald Duck'*, as in duck and hide, or also translated as *'duck'* equals *'fuck'*, as in *'let's get the fuck outta here'*.

'Dock Asthma' – drying up whilst giving evidence in court or losing your nerve – rumour has it that the most severe case of this reported entailed an officer, at a particularly sticky moment in the **'box'**, pretending to faint and being taken off on a stretcher.

'Dodger' – a work-shy individual who avoids jobs and doesn't answer the radio.

'Dodo' – nickname for a lethargic officer who appears as if life is extinct.

'Doing time' – serving a prison sentence – a saying often tendered to younger aspiring criminals by *'older lags'* is, *'if you can't do the time, don't do the crime'*.

'Dole Office' – Unemployment Benefits Office.

'Domestic' – a domestic violence incident.

'Done a runner' – escaped.

'Donkey Wallopers' – mounted police officers.

Figure 2: 'Donkey Wallopers' at the 'footie'

'Do one' – leave immediately.

'Door Slammers' – traffic officers.

'Dose' – venereal disease.

'Double-Bubble' – short notice rest-day working - 'double time' overtime.

'Double-crewed' – a patrol vehicle with two officers.

'Down the steps' – a prisoner when taken down from the dock in court after sentence – judges really do often say *'take him down'* after sentencing.

'Dream Factory' – Lloyd House Police Headquarters – this is the place where the lowly P.C. believes that the senior police leadership 'float around in the clouds' dreaming up new schemes, most of which have been reinvented from failed schemes years previously and yet are re-badged on the basis of *'what comes around goes around.'*

'Drop it on their toes' – put the facts to a suspect and challenge them to admit the offence. Often prefaced by the words, *'I put it to you'*.

'Dropped a clanger' – made a mistake.

'Drum' – a suspect's house.

'Dudley Barbed Wire Act' – where an officer knows

a suspect has done something wrong, but is not quite sure exactly what the offence is, so takes the suspect in and works it out by the time they get to the Custody Officer.

'Due Care' – driving without due care and attention.

'Duplicate key' – a crowbar.

'Dust Up' – a fight.

***

E – Echo

'Early Turn/Earlies' – the early morning shift.

'E's' – ecstasy tablets.

'Electric soup' – whisky.

'Eyeball' – To have sight of a target individual or premises.

'Examine the back of your eyelids' – sleeping whilst on duty.

'Ex's' – expenses.

***

F – Foxtrot

'F.L.I.N.T.S' – Force Linked Intelligence System - computerised software for criminal intelligence analysis involving criminals and suspects.

'FLUB' – a nickname that stands for *'Fat, Lazy, Useless, Bastard'*.

'F.R.' – further written report/update on a crime – late 'FR's' were the downfall of many an aspiring probationary constable.

'F.S.A' – *'Fucking Silly Answer'*.

'Fairy Dell' – cell.

'Fawlty Towers' – Lloyd House, Police HQ, where the Command Team are based.

'Figures 12' – fatal Road Traffic Accident.

'Filing cabinet' – a rubbish bin – useful for mouldering paperwork, as in, *'I've filed it'*.

'First-Timer' – a person with no previous convictions.

'First Watch' – the early turn – a very old term pre-dating organised policing, 'Watchmen' date back to medieval times and even earlier - also **'Late Watch'** and **'Night Watch'** for the other shifts.

'Fizzer' – an internal discipline charge.

'Flasher' – person who is in the habit of indecently exposing his manhood.

'Force of a thousand macs' – a reference to the disparate number of police raincoats worn by officers following the amalgamation of several police forces in 1974, which created the West Midlands Police.

Figure 3: Some of the 'Macs' in all their glory!

'Form' – previous convictions.

'Foxtrot Oscar' – go away.

'Freebie' – anything given away free – officers policing events are partial to a **'freebie hunt'**, and these can get quite competitive.

'Frisk' – to search a person.

'Front' – an apparently legal disguise for a criminal enterprise.

'Full File' – comprehensive police file for court.

***

G – Golf

'G.B.H.' – Grievous Bodily Harm.

'Gaffer' – PC's term for an Inspector or above.

'Gardening Leave' – being placed on 'gardening leave' is something of a 'twilight zone', falling between compassionate leave, sick leave, annual leave and suspension. Usually following a difficult incident when it is decided for whatever reason that an officer is better off away from work, for the good of themselves, and/or the organisation. It can last for a long time, if all parties find it a satisfactory solution whilst a problem is worked through.

'Getting your hands dirty' – dealing with difficult roles and incidents in policing, and/or spending a lot of one's career in operational roles.

'Get sweet F.A.' – get nothing.

'Get your coat' – retired officer Norman Langford recalls, *"When arresting prostitutes in the Varna Road/Princess Road houses in the 60's and 70's, the*

27

girls were always told 'get your coat'. This signified to them all that they were going to be arrested. I recall one occasion when one of the girls complained about a man purporting to be a police officer telling her she was under arrest for not allowing him to have free sex with her. When she was asked how she knew he wasn't a police officer she said, "He didn't tell me to get my coat."...'

'Giggle Stick' – a shortened truncheon which was issued to female officers circa 1976 after the enactment of the Sex Discrimination Act meant that women police officers could go on the *'front line'* - hitherto they had tended to be in departments such as 'children and families'. The problem was that they had no police issue trousers, and skirts had no truncheon pocket. The compromise was the issue of a mini-truncheon that fitted in the uniform issue handbag. Alas it served no practical purpose whatsoever and bore an unfortunate resemblance to a sex aid.

'Give it some welly' – put some effort into it.

'Give us a bell' – phone me.

'Giving some love' – applying Home Office approved techniques in restraint, when dealing with violent prisoners. These techniques replaced the *'clip round the ear'* beloved of older members of the public.

'Going down' – sentenced to imprisonment.

'Go-fer' – someone given menial tasks to do.

'Go for a dump' – use the toilet. One unsolved crime from the annals of West Midlands Police was the identity of *'the phantom log layer'* of Bradford Street Police Station. The rest is best left to the imagination, although, because of the many years this heroic effort continued, it is suspected that the mantle was handed on to other initiates. The diet required remains a closely guarded secret, although curry and beer probably feature.

'Go for a slash' – use the urinal.

'Going for a 'gypsies'' – go to the urinal.

'Gold' –overall police commander at a major incident or event.

'Go nap' – arrest someone.

'Gong' – medal.

'Got potted at court' – found guilty at court of an offence.

'Grab A Grannie Nights' – the nickname for functions at the Tower Ballroom in Edgbaston, Birmingham, routinely attended by officers on courses at the nearby Tally Ho! Police Training

Centre. CID course members were the main habituates. The Tower, now sadly closed, remained in an early Seventies time warp throughout the Eighties, Nineties and later, along with many of its original denizens. It was quite possible, even in later years, to see men with white suits, and shirts open to the navel, sporting large medallions on chains, getting down to some disco dancing. There was also an old joke about some of the women taking out their false teeth, but for the sake of propriety we won't go into that any further.

'Graded Grain' – a Grade One Advanced level police driver.

'Grass' – an informant – as in, *'whispering grass'*. Also *'grass him up',* inform on someone.

'Gripping the rail' – being in court, usually applied to an officer who is being prosecuted for something.

'Grounded' – not allowed to drive police vehicles.

'Ground bait' – someone indicating they are unwell during the shift prior to going sick on their next one.

'Growler' – a police dog – members of the public might anticipate that police dogs are trained to ignore officers and only to be unpleasant towards members of the criminal fraternity. This is not the case. Probationers used to have to *'help'* train the dogs by running for them with a heavily padded arm held out for the dog, hopefully, to attach itself to. This was an unnerving experience, as five stone of excited and slavering German Shepherd rocketed towards one. The practice would have given a modern Health and Safety representative an instant heart attack. So, instead of trying to train the dogs to discriminate between *'goodies'* and *'baddies'*, the advice to officers at a scene when a dog was released in pursuit was to, *'stand perfectly still and hold your balls'*. We don't know what they said to the women. This didn't exactly inspire confidence either, but in reality, the dogs continue to be a valued colleague in all sorts of situations, and having the rear end of one between you and a violent crowd, or person, remains a good place to be.

Figure 4. The 'business end' of a 'growler'

'Guff' – information.

'Gurkha' – a police officer who never takes a prisoner – named after the fearsome Nepalese fighting Regiment that were rumoured to *'take no prisoners'* in battle.

'Gypsies warning' – warned about behaviour – this is a widely-known phrase allegedly derived from a popular 1864 tune, *'The Gypsy's Warning'* in which a gypsy warns a woman away from the *'cad'* who is wooing her - because he had ruined the gypsy's daughter - driving her to her death. The song was apparently very well known in the UK and the US.

***

H – Hotel

'H.M.I.C.' – Her Majesty's Inspectorate of Constabularies.

'HORTI' – a ticket issued requesting the production of driving documents, which is also known as a **'producer'**.

'Half-Blues' – in uniform 'shirt sleeves' and trousers and not wearing a tie. This dates from when issue shirts were blue for Constable and Sergeant ranks.

'Hands up' – an admission of guilt by an offender.

'Handler' - a person who handles stolen goods, also referred to as a *'fence'*. This term is also used to describe a police officer that *'handles'* informants.

'Handover' – dealing with another officer's prisoner. When paid overtime was plentiful, having a prisoner usually meant staying on duty and earning overtime whilst completing the enquiry, sorting out the paperwork, and other necessities. This was unless it was for a serious crime, when the prisoner could be left for the CID, who would often complain about how useless the *'woolies'* or *'woodentops'* were at investigation and paperwork.

When police finances became stretched the *'handover'* was invented. This meant that when you came on duty, you might find yourself dealing with a prisoner who had been arrested by somebody else. The arresting officer was usually off duty and routinely non- contactable. The prisoner would come equipped with a *'handover package'*, ranging from the brilliant, which was rare, to the *'bag of rats'*, which, alas, was very common. Subsequently, whole units were invented to deal with other people's prisoners, in an effort to keep the rapidly diminishing amount of operational officers out on the streets.

This process did bring an element of efficiency in dealing with volume, but personal ownership of an investigation evaporated faster than the most senior officer at a rowdy police social function.

'Hats off and into the crowd' – the traditional British police tall helmet may look both imposing and comforting, although not necessarily comfortable, but it is almost impossible to retain it on one's *'bonce'* in any sort of fight. Thus, this saying refers to wading into a melee, when the helmet would instantly fall off.

'Hats off and mingle' – this one is diametrically opposed to the one above. If outnumbered, remove the helmet and skulk around until backup arrives.

'Have a word in your shell-like' – telling someone to behave by having a one-to-one conversation, usually on a one-way basis, and normally very direct in nature and content.

'Have it away' – stealing something.

'Having a lie down' – remanded or detained in custody – this relates to prisoners being held in police cells overnight. A **'lie down'** can be a sleep period required by law during the first twenty-four hours following arrest, or a remand back to police cells, pre-charge, by a court for further questioning and investigation, called a, **'three-day lie down'**. The latter is usually for protracted, complicated or serious offences to allow for sufficient investigation and evidence gathering.

'Having it' – the offender is confessing. As opposed to the **'full and frank denial'** often experienced, especially after a consultation with a solicitor.

'Having it large' – someone, usually an officer, has fallen for a trick or *'blag'*.

'Headache stick' – a truncheon – and not because it relieves headaches! This must be a very old saying because Home Office guidance is to aim for shins and arms, and never someone's head!

'Heavy Begging' – street robberies.

'Hit' – a good result from a forensic submission.

'Hobby Bobby' – a Special Constable, the volunteer police officers who selflessly give up their time to assist the regulars.

'Holab Forms' – Home Office Laboratory forms - these accompany items submitted for forensic examination.

'Hope you are not in any Xmas Clubs' – You will be in prison for Christmas.

'Hoolie' – a football hooligan.

'Horrorhead' – an officer who is deemed to be less than attractive.

'How long have you got in' – how much service have you got? When grey hairs appear this quickly turns

into, *'how long have you got left?'* Every police officer has two items of information branded into their souls, their joining / retirement date and their collar number.

***

I – India

'Iffy' – something questionable.

'In for snap' – break time, *'snap'* being food. Also *'in for refs'*

'In the hat' – under consideration.

'It's a fair cop' – caught fair and square.

'It's all off at Haydock' – a big fight has broken out.

'It's jam sandwiches for you for breakfast' – no bail for a prisoner.

***

J – Juliet

'J.D.R.' – Juvenile Detention Room.

'Jaffas' – a nickname for any senior officers that were large and round, and had *'pips'* on their shoulders.

'Jam sandwich' – a white police patrol car with red stripe along the side.

'Job' – serving or having served in the police - e.g. **'He/She's Job'**

'Jockeys' – mounted police officers.

'Joint' – a cannabis spliff.

'Jump seat' – the seat nearest to the sliding door in a police van – probationary constables are often allotted this seat as it means that they are first out of the van at an incident, which is viewed as 'character-forming'.

***

K – Kilo

'K.I.V.' – Keep in view.

'Keep ahead of the game' – stay one step ahead.

'Kipper' – 'two-faced and gutless'.

'Kit and kaboodle' – the whole thing. Comes from the old English word 'caboodle' meaning a group or collection of things or people

'Kiting' – presenting stolen cheques in order to commit fraud.

***

L – Lima

'LOBNOD' – retired officer Graeme Pallister recalls the origins of this phrase, *'When resulting a job on the old green screen command and control system the word 'LOBNOD' was often used at Bournville Lane Police Station back in the 80s. It stood for – Load Of Bollocks No Offences Disclosed!'*

'L.O.M.B.A.R.D' – a nickname meaning 'Loads Of Money But A Right Dick'.

'Landline' – the use of a telephone by the police control room to pass a secure message rather than using radio.

'Laptop' – nickname for a small P.C after height restrictions on entrants were removed.

'Lardy' or **'Lardhead'** – derogatory term used by Birmingham officers to refer to their colleagues in the Black Country.

'Leg it' – run away.

'Legend' – the cover story for an undercover officer – relied upon when interrogated or pressured by criminals, or to establish a realistic character in order to infiltrate a criminal enterprise.

'Leg up' – to assist a colleague.

'Lift someone' – to arrest someone.

'Light fingered' – a thief.

'Load of tat' – cheap property.

'Lock–in' – drinking in licensed premises after the doors have been locked to the public.

'Lock-up' – Central Lock Up in Steelhouse Lane. This holding cell complex for Victoria Law Courts is a mini, perfectly formed Victorian prison. It is now no longer operational, but has been preserved for future generations with Lottery and self-generated funding and is open to the public on a regular basis with the help of volunteers.

Figure 5: Inside 'Lock-Up'

'Lowlife' – a lifestyle criminal.

M – Mike

'M.O.' – 'modus operandi' – a Latin phrase that translates as, *'method used'*. In this context it means the method used to commit the crime.

'M.O.B.' – Minor Occurrence Book – was a real book, now long defunct, in which incidents that did not make the grade as recorded crimes were recorded.

'M.S.D. – Music, Singing and Dancing' – the Management Services Department in West Midlands Police HQ, and much beloved by the frontline officers – not!

'MUPPET' – the *'Most Useless Prat the Police Ever Trained'*. Just out of interest, *'Prat'* is a very old English word for trick or cunning that seems to have gone via *'pratting about'* to emerge as meaning 'a fool' in the 1900's.

'Ma'am' – the formal form of address to a female senior officer.

'Margarine Legs' – a derogatory term used to describe a female who frequently had sex. It originated from an old advert that used to claim that margarine spreads much easier than butter.

'Markers' – warning markers on PNC (Police

National Computer), about an individual e.g. 'carries weapons'.

'Mason' – a Freemason.

'Mensa' – someone who is a bit slow on the uptake – sometimes also referred to as **'Bamber'** , after Bamber Gascoigne, the original host of 'University Challenge'.

'Meths' – crystal methadone.

'Micro manage' – to closely supervise.

'Minworth' – a nickname, after the location of the sewage treatment works to describe a person who is *full of shit'*.

'Misper' – Missing person.

'Mod Plod' – Ministry of Defence Police.

'Mogadon' – a *'slow acting dope'*.

'Moniker' – someone's name or nickname.

'More form than Arkle' – lots of previous convictions, named after the champion racehorse.

'Morning Prayers' – retired officer Conrad Szamocki recalls this as, *'having an alcoholic drink on a Monday morning at 6am after finishing seven straight night duties',* whilst another officer, Tony Griffiths, recalls this as also being referred to as *'Choir practice'*. The phrase *'Morning Prayers',* was also more recently used to define early morning briefing sessions between senior officers on crime and incidents that had occurred in the preceding twenty-four hours.

'Moth' – an officer drawn to the lights of the police station.

'Mowgli' – an officer *'lost in the urban jungle'*.

'Mufti' – in plain clothes rather than uniform. It originates from the British Army in the early nineteenth century and is thought to stem from the Arabic word for a scholar. These people wore robes or gowns and this mode of off-duty dress – dressing gown, tasselled cap and slippers, is reputed as having been adopted by British officers at the time.

'Mug-shot' – a facial photograph of person in custody.

'My office straight away' – in big trouble with a senior officer.

***

N – November

'NARPO' – National Association of Retired Police Officers.

'N.F.A.' – No Fixed Abode – otherwise known as *'no fresh air'* as such a prisoner would not normally be granted bail if arrested.

'N.F.A' – no further action – released without charge.

'N.F.I.' – *'no fucker in'* – when knocking a door and getting no answer. Retired officer Jeff Barley recalls a slightly more polite version, *'when questioned by a Judge at court what an entry in the SOCO job book meant when it said 'NFI' the officer replied 'No Fellows In' to the amusement of the Judge who smiled in disbelief.'*

'N.H.W.' – Neighbourhood Watch.

'NOD' – No Offences Disclosed.

'NTOA' – No Trace On Arrival.

'Negative' – No.

'Nigel' – an instrument for forcing doors open. Retired police officer David Faulkner tells the following story, *'From the Drug Squad. Now I know it's developed since then, but here is the real story. We needed a ram to enter reinforced premises. Sledgehammers didn't cut the mustard. Nick Batsford approached a foundry and they came up with a two-man ram. It was supplied and painted enamel black. We called it 'Nigel' after the boxer Nigel Benn aka,*

'the dark destroyer'. Things move on and little red rams containing sliding internal barring were supplied and to this day 'Nigel' is still used as the slang word for the tool'.

'Nigerian Lager' – Guinness.

'Niggle' – a card game habitually played during refreshments.

'Nonce' – a sex offender – this is actually criminal slang adopted by the police. It is possibly originally from dialectal '*nonce, nonse'*, a *'stupid, worthless individual'*, or, '*nance',* an, *'effeminate man'*, from '*Nancy boy'*.

***

O – Oscar

'O.S.U.' – Operational Support Unit – the West Midlands Police version of the *'Special Patrol Group',* **'serials'** of officers specially trained to deal with riot and public order situations. They were legendary within **'the Job'** for their professionalism, courage, humour and practical jokes.

Figure 6: A 'PSU' of the 'OSU - three 'Serials'

'O.T.' – overtime – linked to the saying, *'the golden goose has crapped'.*

'Oaksey breaks' – retired officer Derek Rowe recalls that this phrase came about in reference to the taking of refreshment breaks following a review into police pay and conditions by Lord Oaksey in 1960.

'Old Sweat' – a long-serving officer.

'Old Chestnut' – a story which has been told over and over again.

'Olympic Torch' – nickname for an officer believed to never leave the station. It never goes out....

'One and Ten' – a public order *'serial'* of ten officers with a sergeant. This is the standard basic deployment configuration. Three **'one and tens'** make up a **'PSU'** - Police Support Unit. (See our book, 'The Noble

Cause' for a whole chapter on public order).

'On remand' – awaiting trial or sentence at court.

'On the carpet' – receiving a 'telling off' by a senior officer.

'On the game' – engaging in prostitution.

'On the hurry up' – done quickly.

'On the roundabout' – attending various courses and attachments one after the other.

'On the Magic Roundabout' – going around in circles.

'On the sheet' – recording the details of an arrested person. The **'sheet'** is the 'person in custody' record, a large-sized pre-printed template, now of course computerised, but the term continues.

'On their toes' – criminals running away.

'On your way in' -A much dreaded phrase coming over the radio. It's the end of the shift and the Controller (who probably has a grudge from something you've done earlier), has 'one quick job' to sort before you finish. Normally this will take several hours to sort.

'One too many' – under the influence of alcohol.

'Op Order' – a written operational order.

'Out of his skull' – drunk.

'Oppo' – police partner when double-crewed.

***

P – Papa

'PADFA' – Police Arrived Did Fuck All.

'P.B.O.' – Permanent Beat Officer – an officer assigned to work a fixed beat for a significant period of time, usually months or years.

'P.B.T.' – a positive breath test.

'P.D.R.' – Personal Development Review – the annual appraisal process.

'P.I.C.' – person in custody.

'P.N.B.' – pocket notebook.

'P.N.C' – Police National Computer.

'P.S.U.' – Police Support Unit – comprised of three **'one-tens'** or **'serials'**, so thirty constables, three sergeants, one inspector and three vans.

'Panda' – local police patrol vehicle.

'Patch' – police area or beat.

'Pay a visit' – go to the toilet.

'Pay Day Discos' – Legendary disco's held at the Tally Ho! Police Training Centre for staff on paydays.

'P.B. Entry' – an entry in an officer's police pocket notebook, detailing their recollection of an incident. These notes are written up as soon as possible after the incident, whilst the memory is fresh. A classic joke relates to a police officer in the witness box who when asked under cross examination, 'and when did you make your notes up, officer?' Replied. *'They're not made up, they're the truth!'*

'PC Rain' – a police officer's best friend, that guaranteed a quiet shift. Often prayed for in riot situations which you may observe always seem to take place on hot summer days, after all, who wants to riot on a miserable, wet, British day?

'Peewee' – a policewoman.

'Peg' – a wooden truncheon. Also the verb, **to peg'.**

'Peterman' – a person who specialised in *'blowing'* safes with explosives.

'Pick up an enclosure' – to run an errand whilst on duty – sometimes official, more often to do with milk, bacon sandwiches etc.

'Pimp' – a person who controls prostitutes, often via violence and drugs.

'Pinks' – Force Orders. Actually printed on pink paper, these documents detailed promotions, moves, resignations, retirements and disciplinary findings, and their reading was often accompanied by outbursts of, *'you'll never believe which wanker they've promoted now!'*.

'Pink Slips' – pink slip inserts at the back of 'flip over' police pocketbooks, used for aide- memoires. Retired officer Derek Rowe recalls jokingly that, *'the slips were also used to issue unofficial 'official extensions' to pub licensees who at that time had to close at 10pm.'*

'Pips' – 'bath stars' worn on uniforms to denote ranks above sergeant – two for an Inspector, and three for a Chief Inspector

Figure 7: The 'Pips' are on the left and next to the Crown

'Pissing in the same pot' – a joint venture.

'Pissing themselves' – can't stop laughing.

'Plan B's – coming on later on early shift, or leaving early on nights, organised within each shift by rota, usually to use up some of the vast amounts of *'time owing'* accrued by officers, who would otherwise have to be paid for them.

'Plank' – a somewhat dim person.

'Played a blinder' – did a good job.

'Playing the pink trombone' – two males engaged in fellatio in a public toilet.

'Plonk' – a historical derogatory term for a female police officer – unsurprisingly no longer used, it allegedly stands for *'Person of Little Or No Knowledge'*. If you've watched *'Life On Mars'* you will get an idea of the attitudes towards female officers in the past. It is true, but society was like it too.

'Poets Day' – a shift worker's view of Police Headquarters staff on a Friday – it stands for, *'Piss Off Early, Tomorrow's Saturday'*.

'Polacc' – a road traffic accident involving a police vehicle – this always leads to reams of paperwork for the duty Sergeant.

'Porky Pies' – lies.

'Positive I.D.' – confirmed identification of suspect.

'Prints' – fingerprints.

'Process' – reporting someone by way of summons, as opposed to charge – this basically means that the relevant court would *'summon'* the offender.

'Producer' – a form requiring the production of driving documents.

'Pro-Con' – police officer with under two years' service – also known as *'teamaker'*.

'Pros Sols' – Prosecuting Solicitor – this role pre-dates the Crown Prosecution Service.

'Pulling a flanker' – tricking someone, or circumventing rules and procedure.

'Punched, Bored and countersunk' – *don't know which way to turn as too busy.'*

'Put it to him' – *To put the facts of the case to a person suspected of committing an offence with a view to obtaining a confession.''*

'Put the ticket in' – to retire.

'Put Up' – retired officer Roger Baker remembers

this phrase as being *'A place on a beat such as a residence, business premises, pub, fire station, or café where you were welcome to rest for tea, coffee or a pint!'*

'Putting a good word in for someone' – retired officer Mick Ferris remembers this phrase from the days when police officers often presented their own cases at court as, *'attending court on a guilty plea to say something positive about the defendant to the magistrates before they were sentenced'. This became a formalised process in later years to prevent 'deals' being done.*

'Put on the sheet' – being reported for a discipline offence, also known as being, **'stuck on'**.

***

Q – Quebec

'Q.P.M.' – Queen's Police Medal.

'Qualified' – the individual has passed a promotion examination. These examinations only apply to Sergeant and Inspector rank, and do not guarantee promotion.

'Q word' – all quiet – nothing is happening – but don't say the word otherwise something will happen. Something akin to mentioning *'the Scottish play'* in the theatre.

'Queens Half Hour' – an unpaid half an hour at the end of a shift before paid overtime kicked in – we never minded doing a bit for Her Majesty!

Figure 8: Her Majesty thanking Michael Layton for all those half hours.

'Quick-changeover' – off duty at 10pm and back on duty at 6am. The first three hours of the subsequent early shift were conducted in a buzz of adrenalin, but once a *'big belly breakfast'* was consumed, the slump set in. Opinions were divided as to the merits of not actually sleeping at all between these shifts, with some of the livelier officers using quick changeover as an opportunity for a night out, sometimes with the inclusion of sleeping in the station. This was because, by the time commuting, finishing late and arriving early enough to be ready for parade were removed from the eight hour gap between shifts, the opportunity for sleep could be as little as four hours

anyway.

***

R – Romeo

'R.I.C.' – remand in custody.

'R.T.A' – Road Traffic Accident.

'Radial Roads' – these were restricted main roads into Birmingham with no parking between 7.30am and 9am, and 4.30pm and 6pm daily.

'Rat-arsed' – drunk.

'Rat Run' – a favoured escape route for a criminal trying to get back home.

'Rattler' – the train.

'Rattle off' – provide the relevant information.

'Reception Committee' – a group of officers waiting at the custody block, to assist with the restraint of a particularly violent prisoner being brought into the station.

'Red-Ink' – entries in police diaries and pocket books relating to expenses/payments made to informants.

'Refs' – refreshment break.

'Reg number' – vehicle registration plate.

'Rent Boy' – a young male prostitute.

'Resident Bike' – a female who is well known in an area for being sexually liberated.

'Ribbing' – teasing.

'Right Bell-End' – an idiot.

'Right scrote' – unsavoury character – derived from the word scrotum.

'Ringer' – a stolen vehicle on false plates – **'Its been rung'** means that the engine and chassis numbers have been changed, together with the plates, and often with false documentation provided in more sophisticated operations.

'Ring Stinger' – a very hot curry – often accompanied the next day by a rendition of Johnny Cash's *'Ring of Fire'* from all participants.

'Rolling Over' – a suspect admitting their guilt during interview – alternatively known as a **'cough'**.

'Rubber-Heel Squad' – the Complaints and Discipline Department – so-called because of their ability to creep up on an officer unheard!

'Run them through the box' – check a person on

PNC for criminal records.

'Runner' –a custody assistant in the cell block – once an officer, now they are police staff or from a private company.

'RV Point' – rendezvous point – mostly used for firearms jobs or major incidents and events.

***

S – Sierra

'S.B.' – Special Branch.

'S.F.Q's' – silly fucking questions – beloved of trainers of police officers who could be sure someone would ask something ridiculous every time. Some officers excelled at being bloody- minded by posing ever more unlikely scenarios to the exasperation of the trainer.

'S.H.L.P.S.' – Steelhouse Lane Police Station.

'S.I.D.S' – Sudden Infant Death Syndrome or **'Cot Death'**.

'S.L.O.B' – a nickname, *'Slow, Lazy, Obnoxious Bastard'*.

'S.O.C.O.' – Scenes Of Crime Officer.

'S.T.S.' – Shop theft squad – shoplifters are a

particular scourge of city-centre custody blocks, due to their numbers, so specialist squads were formed to deal with the paperwork.

'Sarbut' – a police informant – retired officer Jeff Barley recalls this word being used as one of the questions on the quiz programme, *'Call My Bluff'* hosted by Robert Robinson when the word was described as being in the English dictionary as being a Midlands police term. The only theory as to origin that we have found is that it is a shortened version of *'saboteur'*.

'Sarge' – Sergeant.

'Screaming Skull' – a nickname for a less than handsome officer.

'Scruffies' – police motorcyclists – from the days when the neatness of appearance in tunic, trousers, shirt, tie and helmet was considered important. The bikers of course got to wear leathers and waterproofs.

'Scumbag' – a troublemaker or low-life.

'Secret Squirrels' – Police Complaints Department – also used for the Security Services.

'Section 18' – a serious offence of wounding with intent. (Offences Against Person Act 1861).

'Section 20' – an offence of wounding without intent.

(OAP Act).

'Section 39' – common assault. (OAP Act).

'Section 47' – assault occasioning actual bodily harm. (OAP Act).

'Section 47(3)' – on police bail. (Police and Criminal Evidence Act).

'Scaffed' – when the ignition barrel of a car had been broken prior to its theft. Stems from the past when scaffolding bars were used to steal cars.

'Scrambled Egg' – the adornments of oak-leaves on the epaulettes of very senior officers.

'Scribe' – person taking interview notes or writing a witness or defendant's statement.

'Script' – pocket-book evidence entry.

'Scruffs' – police officers in casual plain clothes.

'Scuffler' – city-centre fighting type – usually a drunk/football hooligan.

Figure 9: A 'Scuffler's' Business Card.

'Section 5' – threatening, abusive, or insulting behaviour. (Public Order Act).

'Shaking Handles' – Trying shop door handles to make sure that the premises were secure – the stuff of Dixon of Dock Green!

'Shagger' – someone who has sex with different men or women on a frequent basis – is applicable to either sex.

'Shebang' – the whole issue.

'Shennanigins' – causing trouble, or up to no good.

'Shiny arse' – an officer who works in an office full time.

'Shiv' – a knife – a prison slang term, often used for a blade manufactured from items to hand **'inside'**.

'Short arms, deep pockets' – reluctant to buy a round of drinks at the bar.

'Sideboards' / 'Sideburns' – facial hair favoured by police officers in the 70s – along with cowboy boots and *'Jason King'* moustaches in the CID. A corruption of the word 'Burnside's' after American Civil War General Ambrose Burnside, who was renowned for this style of facial hair.

Figure 10: 'Life On Mars'? A fashion - conscious CID officer in the 70's sporting 'Sideboard's or 'Sideburns'.

'Silver' – strategic police commander at a major

incident or event.

'Shirt Sleeve Order' – a permitted dress code of no tunic, just shirt. If the shirts was short sleeved an open neck/ no tie was permitted. Reserved for the hottest weather

'Shout' – call for urgent assistance by an officer.

'Silent approach' – instruction to attend a job without sirens/horns/lights or park up short and walk so as not to alert the criminal to the approach of police.

'Slap head' – bald person – also called **'Bald Eagle'**, after the *'Muppet Show'* character.

'Slip them a crippler' – ask a difficult question in interview.

'Slippery customer' – evasive.

'Snap' – food taken during refreshment break.

'Snitch' – an informant.

'Snotted' – punched.

'Snowdropper' – thief who steals (ladies) underwear from clothing lines – this is a surprisingly common activity.

'Snout' – an informant.

'Solicitors Runner' – person who sits in on police interviews representing a client on behalf of a solicitor – they are often retired police officers, who are generally more difficult than the actual solicitor as they know all the *'tricks of the trade'*.

'Special' – Special Constable.

'Spent' – an expired criminal conviction that no longer appears on a criminal record.

'Spent withs' – expenses claim for money spent with informants.

'Spin the drum' – search a prisoner's house.

'Spinning' – whistling or shouting at someone from a van to make them turn around, then all looking away – a favourite trick of the **OSU**.

'Spit the dummy out of the pram' – get upset – otherwise known as **'throwing a teddy in the corner'**.

'Split-Arses' – an old derogatory term for females. (We thought long and hard about including this one, but it is a part of police culture and history, and evidences the long journey our female colleagues have made to the very top of policing.)

'Springer' – someone who buys the drinks for others at the bar.

'Sprog' – *a* Probationary Constable.

'Stand down' – conclude an operation or duty.

'Standing By' – waiting.

'Stanley' – a Stanley Knife when used as a weapon.

'Station bike' – a policewoman with an open-minded attitude to sexual encounters.

'Station candle' – an officer who rarely goes out.

'Station cat' – an officer who rarely goes out – otherwise known as **'Corky'**.

'Steady Eddie' – officers who take their time to do things and are generally risk averse.

'Stick' – an Inspector – believed to originate from the *'night stick'* carried by Inspectors in days of old.

'Sticky wicket' – not on safe ground in terms of giving an account of an event.

'Stipe' – Stipendiary Magistrate at Law Courts.

Figure 11: Victoria Law Courts, Birmingham

'Stop Form' – Stop and Search forms.

'Stop Vehicle Seen' – a form used to record the details of vehicles stopped mainly on night duties.

'Stuck on' – put on an internal discipline charge.

'Sudden death' – any death, whether sudden or expected.

'Suited and booted' – looking smart.

'Supergrass' – a protected informant in an organised crime enquiry.

'Supt' – Superintendent.

'Swallow it' – to believe something.

'**Swift one**' – a quick alcoholic drink – unfortunately for spouses, this often turned into, '**a session**', and later into a divorce!

'**Swinging the Blue Lamp**' – older officers reminiscing about *'the good old days'*.

'**Sword of Zorro**' – retired police officer Jeffrey Barley recalls from his days as a Scenes of Crime Officer, *' When having done a scene of crime fingerprint examination correctly we then put lots of fingerprint powder on it to make it obvious that we had done the job!'*

***

T – Tango

'**T.A.**' – time of arrival at an incident recorded on a log - also referred to as '**Plus T.A.**', because that was the code typed onto the computer log, (+TA).

'**T.A.D.A.**' – Unauthorised take and drive away of a motor vehicle.

'**T.D.R.**' – temporarily medically restricted from operational duties.

'**T.F.M.V.**' – theft from motor vehicle.

'**T.I.C.**' – an offence taken into consideration at court.

'T.I.T.S' – a nickname, *'Too Idle To Shit'*.

'T.O.I.L.' – time-off in lieu.

'Taking a bending' – having a heavy workload.

'Taking a bung' – a corrupt payment to an officer.

'Taking a hostage' – the arrest of a family member to encourage someone wanted by the police to give themselves up.

'Taking a grilling' – an intensive cross-examination by a defence barrister or solicitor at court.

'Tatters' – people who look for scrap metal.

'Tay on we' – it's not on our police area – a Black Country term that spread to Birmingham. There was a practice of writing off incident logs on the computer by typing *'TOW'*, which puzzled many a person not in the know.

'Tea-Leaf' – thief.

'Teflon' - an officer skilled or lucky in escaping work or problems – *'nothing sticks'*.

'Text Letter' – confidential letter to a Judge when a registered informant is appearing for sentence – sometimes referred to as a **'script'**.

'The Bench' – magistrate's sitting in court.

'The Big House' – Crown Court.

'The Birmingham Breathing Act' – retired officers Ray Humes and Derek Rowe recall that this referred to a piece of legislation which appeared to allow you to arrest anybody for anything, *The Birmingham Corporation Consolidation Act 1914 gave constables in the City the power to arrest a person for an offence, both summary and indictable, where that person's identity was in doubt, or he refused to give it. This was sometimes also referred to as the 'Cotton Wool Act' the 'Barbed Wire Act', 'Ways and Means Act' and 'Section 1 Dudley Baths Act.*

'The Block' – the cells.

'The Blower' – the telephone. **'The Box'** – giving evidence on oath in court from the witness box. A retired officer recalls that on one occasion a defence barrister asked a CID officer if he was aware what happened if he did not tell the truth under oath. The officer responded, *'Yes a fairy will die.'* Apparently even the Judge had a giggle. On another occasion an officer asked if he could refresh his memory from the record of evidence in his pocket-note-book during a Crown Court case. When asked when he had made his notes up, he responded, *'I didn't make them up. They are true.'*

'The Box' – the Police National Computer.

'The Blue Brick' – the police station.

'The Chief' – Chief Constable.

'The Dep' – Deputy Chief Constable.

'The Digbeth Act' – a fictitious piece of legislation referred to in the Digbeth area

Figure 12: Digbeth Police Station

'The Domino King' – a Judge who dealt with offenders by means of sentencing in three and five years. Apparently one defendant who called the Judge this to his face received four years imprisonment.

'The early morning knock' – the classic early morning arrest/getting someone out of bed.

'The ESSO Squad' – Lloyd House workers – stands for, *'Every Saturday and Sunday Off'*.

'The Green' – Her Majesty's Prison Winson Green –
a Victorian local prison built in 1849 and located in
Winson Green near the centre of Birmingham. A total
of thirty-five judicial executions by way of hanging,
took place at the prison during the 20th century, the
last one being in 1962. Today it holds 1,450 remand
and sentenced prisoners.

WINSON GREEN JAIL, BIRMINGHAM OPENED OCTOBER 1849

Figure 13: 'The Green'

'The Group' – Special Patrol Group.

'The Office' – the police station. Generally a CID
term, as in *'see you back at the office in ten'*.

'The Job' – being in the police – there is something
about having been a police officer that sticks, even
after retirement, and other officers can instinctively

recognise someone as **'Job'**.

'The Lane' – Steelhouse Lane Police Station, Birmingham City Centre – it was built for Birmingham City Police and opened in 1933 as their Central Police Station, replacing a Victorian station on the same site. For around sixty years, until closed in 2005, the station housed a private bar in the basement, allowing officers to drink when not on duty. The station closed on Sunday 15 January 2017.

Figure 14: Steelhouse Lane Police Station.
(Modern photo)

'The Nick' – Police Station.

'The Thursday Gang' – a group of armed robbers who always carried out attacks on a Thursday, the day payroll cash would be delivered to companies for a Friday payment. Before BACS, when little brown wage packets containing cash were the norm.

'The troops' – a number of police officers.

'The Vale' – Castle Vale Police Station.

'The Wood' – Chelmsley Wood Police Station.

'The proof of the pudding is in the eating' – confirmation of the quality of the information will only be known once acted upon and a result known.

'Thief Taker' – an officer with a reputation for making lots of arrests.

'This won't get the babby washed' – not being able to get something important done due to being diverted by something less important – from old Brummie/Black Country slang.

'Three day lie down' – a remand to the cells for three days.

'Throw a sickie' – report sick.

'Tin tack' – getting the sack.

'Tit Hat' – the traditional tall police officer's helmet, which rarely fits properly, falls off at the slightest provocation, and is believed to actually mould the head to fit. The name comes from the shape, coupled with the metal cap.

Figure 15: The traditional 'Tit hat'.

'Time -in' or **'Time-served–** officers who are past police retirement age.

'Topped themselves' – committed suicide.

'Torched' – set on fire by an arsonist.

'Tradecraft' –the *'dark art'* of learning how to work undercover or with informants.

'Trap One' – a toilet cubicle.

'Toe-rag' – a criminal – as in *'only fit to wipe your feet with'*.

'Treble 666s' – internal police discipline notice – it was apparently just a coincidence that it is the number of the devil!

'Trot On' – an instruction given to police horses during public order training. This term was also used to encourage people causing trouble to 'go away'.

'Trudge and Wedge' – a public-order training term – given the size and weight of a *'long'* public order shield, trudging is the only option. The wedge is a formation used by a shield party.

'Turkey Trot' – extra van patrols in the Small Heath area of Birmingham to protect butcher's shops in the run up to a Christmas period.

'Turning Queens' or **'Greasy Side Up'** – giving evidence against a co-accused.

'Turning someone or something over' – carrying out a search.

'Two-ten' – the evening shift.

'Twocker' – car thief - derives from **'T.W.O.C'**, *'Taking (a vehicle) Without Consent'*.

***

U – Uniform

73

'U.C.' – Undercover Officer.

'U.S.I.' – unlawful (underage) sexual intercourse.

'Uniform Carrier' – a useless officer.

'Up before the beak' – appearing before the magistrate.

'Urgent Assistance required' – drop everything and go to the assistance of a colleague requiring immediate help, which is not used lightly – even the mention of the word *'assistance'* will provoke a response from colleagues who will attempt to make the scene as soon as possible by any means. A less frenetic response will follow a request for *'back up'*.

***

V – Victor

'Valelites' – Castle Vale residents.

'Verbal' – retired officer Mick Ferris recalls his experiences of this aspect of policing. *'A 'verbal' or the 'verballing' of someone, was about recording alleged comments made by a defendant at the time of their arrest and interview which would then be later denied as having been said after they had spoken to their solicitor!'*

'Villain' – a criminal.

W – Whisky

'W.O.W' – Wanted on Warrant.

'Wacky Races Day' – the day once a month when beat officers drove response vehicles to assist response officer workloads.

'Ways And Means Act' – the officer knows a crime has been committed but is not sure exactly what. It will be sorted out later after reference to the textbooks or online law resource.

'Weed' – cannabis.

'Whanging' – getting hit by multiple pairs of uniform leather gloves – a form of punishment that usually followed an act of stupidity by an officer.

'Wheels' – a vehicle.

'Whingeing' – complaining.

'White despatch' – fetching a bottle of milk.

'White Report' – general report, sometimes called a *'247'*.

'Windy' – a risk averse person.

'Wind-up' – playing a trick or telling a tall story to

achieve a response. The response is called *'a bite'*.

'Winging it' – not preparing, making it up as you go along.

'Wipe your feet on the way out' – after visiting a less hygienic residence where the carpets are sticky and the offer of a cup of tea, if made, is politely refused.

'Wobble-gobs' – people who talk constantly.

'Woodentops' – derogatory CID term for uniform officers.

'Woodies' – Chelmsley Wood residents.

'Woollies' – derogatory CID term for uniform officers, derived from the woolly NATO style jumpers worn.

'Wrap' – a drugs deal, usually wrapped in Clingfilm.

'Write-Offs' – offences admitted by persons serving prison sentences.

***

X – X-Ray

'X4 Intel' – unreliable intelligence.

'X-Ray 1' – the West Midlands Police Mobile Incident Room.

***

Y – Yankee

'Yampy' – stupid or mad – a Black Country term.

'Yam-Yam' – term used by Birmingham officers to describe people from the Black Country.

'Yankee Mike' – West Midlands Police national call sign and Force Control Room radio name.

'Yellow Jersey' – the person doing the most overtime – named after the vest worn by the leader in the Tour de France.

'Yellow Legs' – firefighters.

'Yellow Peril' – a fixed penalty ticket.

'Yobs' – hooligans.

'You'll do, off at 2' – an arrest requiring an officer on nights to go off duty at 2am in order to go to court in the morning, in the days before cases were presented by solicitors. Retired officer Dave Jinks recalls one incident, *'In the days in Birmingham City Police when bobbies were marched to their beats behind the Duty Sergeant, there was the tale of an old 'C' division PC, the first officer following the sergeant, who was back in Lozells Road Station with a prisoner, before the last PC exited to his beat. At* *court the miscreant complained that the arresting officer, on arresting him for being drunk and disorderly, had declared 'You'll do...off at two'. In those days officers had to give evidence at court for any arrest and would be allowed to book off at 2am to give such evidence'.*

'Your name was mentioned' – informed on as being a suspect for a crime.

***

Z – Zulu

'Zulu Cars' – fast-response police vehicles from the Sixties onwards - as in the T.V series *'Z cars'*.

Acknowledgements/References

The following serving, and retired, police officers from the West Midlands Police, British Transport Police and other Forces are especially thanked for their interest and support in the development of this project – we had some fun doing it! :

Jeffrey Barley, Roger Baker, Bob Bird, Andy Brizell, Chris Butler, Ray Calladine, Phil Christie, Brian Churm, Graeme Clark, Jason Clarke, Mike Cresswell, Andy Crowson, Barry Crowley, Conrad Szamocki, David Faulkner, Steve Favill, Mick Ferris, Tony Griffiths, Malcolm (Doc) Halliday, Dave Harris, Adrian (Ada) Howells, Martin Hudson, Ray Humes, Ron James, Dave Jinks, Dave Jisra, Kevin Kelsey, Peter Keys, Stuart Knight, Norman Langford, Bob Lessumun, Ian Mabbett, Mindy Mahil, Julie Maley, Cheryl Moorhouse, Steve Murtagh, Graeme Pallister, Dawn Pinches, Andy Rollason, Derek Rowe, Ken Rowley, Darren Sutton, Ralph Tallis, Teri Timmins, Mat Walker, Pete Walmsley, Andy Watson, Nigel Wier.

A special thanks to **Debbie Menzel** (West Midlands Police Museum Group) for her valued support in relation to visual material.

References from Wikipidia.

A note from the authors

If you enjoyed this book please take a moment to leave a review on its Amazon page. It will be greatly appreciated. If you want to know more about our Brummie/Midlands books, fiction and non-fiction, please visit and *'like'* our Facebook page *'Bostin Books'*. We hope you enjoy them and many thanks for your support.

Michael Layton & Stephen Burrows (July 2018).